profiles

from *In Review*
Canadian Books for Children

compiled by Irma McDonough

Canadian Library Association, Ottawa, 1971

In Review is published quarterly by the Provincial Library Service, 4 New Street, Toronto 5, Ontario

Published by the Canadian Library Association
151 Sparks Street, Ottawa 4, Ontario, Canada
Copyright © 1971 Canadian Library Association
ISBN 0-88802-072-4
Printed and bound in Canada

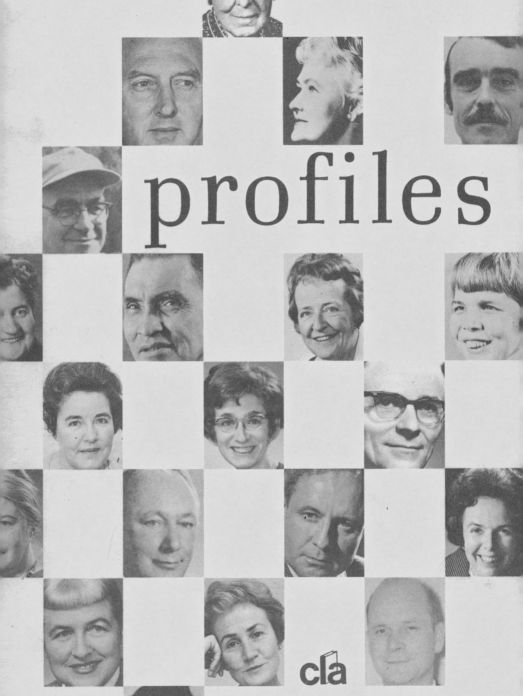

profiles

cla

Contents

Introduction

There had been a need for a review periodical of Canadian books for children for a long time. It took a hundred years to fill the need for a National Library, but we finally got *it* in 1967, and *In Review* started publication that year too.

Canadian librarians with whom I discussed the project in 1966 responded enthusiastically to the idea of a review periodical. And a talk with my director, Bill Roedde, placed the onus for a critical reviewing medium on Ontario's Department of Education, with permission to start one in the Provincial Library Service. A committee of Ontario librarians, Elaine de Temple, Callie Israel, Elinor Kelly, Ruth Osler, and Dorothy Reid helped to decide on the scope of the periodical. And I have tried ever since to respond to the need, the responsibility and the scope with the highest of professional standards.

Along with critical reviews and articles, Profiles have appeared in *In Review* right from the first issue. They are descriptive and biographical rather than critical, although a measure of adulation is bound to creep in. The librarian-profilers interview their subjects and often make new friends this way. Some of the Profiles are written in French and appear with English translations. This practice follows *In Review* policy to deal with Canadiana written in both our official languages, with reviews, articles and Profiles written in either language.

I welcome the Canadian Library Association's decision to anthologize the 20 Profiles that appear in *In Review's* first four years of production. I hope the booklet will find a welcome place in many libraries – in Canada and abroad.

Irma McDonough
Editor, In Review

Claude Aubry

An alabaster bust stands on a shelf behind Claude Aubry's office desk. When you find out that it is a bust of Savanarola you are not surprised for Savonarola was a fiery, strong-willed monk who preached reform in mediaeval Florence. Claude Aubry is a reformer too, fiery in his writing, and strong-willed in his work as a librarian. He is a creative person, a civilized man, and he says, "I want to be known as a human being." He thinks war is terrible, and he deplores the present Vietnamese struggle. And he thinks we should not ignore the problems of other people, of other nations. We must know and allow points of view that are different from our own. That is why he is proud to be a Canadian with a difference. Understandably, Claude Aubry admires French-Canadian writers who stand on their own feet and reflect modern French Canada in their writing.

Claude Aubry was born 23 October 1914 in Morin Heights, Quebec where his father worked as a carpenter. His first Canadian ancestor came to New France over three hundred years ago with the famous Regiment de Carignan in the 1640s. A quick tempered Irishman, Cornelius Teague O'Brennan settled on a farm near Montreal with his Parisian wife. Their neighbours soon shortened O'Brennan to Aubry because the former name was too long.

Mr Aubry has charmed many groups of children with talks on his work as an author and about his colourful ancestors and his own youth. He tells them about walking or skiing the two miles to school in clement weather, until his village bought an ox and

1

cart – probably the most unusual school bus! Even then storms often detained the school children at the local railway station where the stationmaster gave them lessons.

From these rural parts Claude Aubry moved on to Montreal where he obtained his B.A. at the University of Montreal in 1936, after having attended the second oldest college in Canada, St Mary's, for classical studies. On graduation he became an accountant in a trust company, and after some years decided that he would prefer library work. He received his degree in library science from McGill in 1946, became chief librarian at Ottawa Public Library in 1953, then in 1965 director of the Eastern Ontario Regional Library System as well.

As a member of several library and literary associations Mr Aubry has held many responsible posts – vice-president of the Canadian Library Association, president of l'Association Canadienne des Bibliothécaires de Langue Française among others.

Claude Aubry has written dozens of radio and television plays for the French network of the CBC, as well as several books in French. *Les Iles du roi Maha Maha II*, translated by Alice Kane as *The King of the Thousand Islands*, won the Canadian Association of Children's Librarians Book of the Year for Children medal in 1962, and the same award in 1965 for *Le Loup de Noël*, translated by Alice Kane as *The Christmas wolf*. The first of these was submitted anonymously in manuscript to a literary contest sponsored by the Canadian Association of Teachers of the French Language (ACELF) and won the first prize award of $500. It is a fantasy about an amorous king of the Thousand Islands in the St Lawrence River. One reviewer said that both medal winners are "works of spare, carefully polished prose, offbeat and humorously compassionate." *The Christmas wolf* tells how the fierce old wolf Griboux helps some Laurentian villagers to appreciate the true spirit of Christmas. Doubleday will publish a new translation of *The King of the Thousand Islands* in the United States in the spring of 1971.

Peter Martin Associates published the English edition of *The Magic fiddler and other legends of French Canada* in 1968 simultaneously with a French edition published by Les Editions des Deux Rives. The book was designed by Carl Dair using his new type face, "Cartier," illustrated by Saul Field, and translated for the English edition by Alice Kane. Doubleday will publish *Agouhanna, brave among the braves* simultaneously in Toronto and New York in 1971. A short novel about an Iroquois boy, it was illustrated by the Aubrys' son, François, and Suzanne and Danielle, his twin sisters, when they were 10 and 11 years old. Mr Aubry reports that his manuscript, *Le Chien transparent*, has been refused by all publishers who have seen it although he says it is his best book and still hopes that it will reach an audience.

Mr Aubry is married to the former Marie Paule St Onge, herself a writer, and a reviewer of books for *Le Chatelaine*. They have seven children – the Aubrys' severest literary critics.

Irma McDonough
Provincial Library Service, Toronto

Clare Bice

A variety of talents are combined with a very genial personality in London, Ontario's Clare Bice. He was significantly and nationally acclaimed in 1952 when he was awarded a fellowship by the Canadian government for a year's study in France. Dr Bice was well known, however, in Canada and beyond long before this time, and through the years the respect and cordial regard in which he is held have been consistently augmented.

Born in Durham, Ontario, 24 January 1909, Clare Bice was educated in London public and secondary school systems and received his BA from the University of Western Ontario after which he studied art at New York Art Students' League and Grand Central School of Art, New York. With the opening of the Elsie Perrin Williams Memorial Building in London in 1940, he was appointed curator of the Art Museum. In 1942 he joined the Canadian army and after service in Canada and Europe resumed this post.

As a landscape painter, portrait artist, book illustrator and curator at the London Public Library and Art Museum, Dr Bice has achieved great renown and to him is given the credit

3

for establishing the Saturday morning art classes for children. This is an extensive educational program in co-operation with city schools and has become a regular feature at the London Public Library and Art Museum and has proven highly successful.

It has been fortunate for readers and librarians alike that several authors of books for children were able to persaude Dr Bice to illustrate their books. Among the results of this collaboration are: Hooke's *Thunder in the mountains,* Mitchell's *Animals, plants and machines,* Longstreth's *The Force carries on,* Good's *At the dark of the moon,* Leitch's *The Great canoe,* Fox's *The Bruce beckons,* Clark's *The Golden pine cone, The Sun horse, The One-winged dragon, The Silver man, The Hunter and the Medicine Man.*

Several others to which he, along with other illustrators, made contributions are: McIntosh's *Adventure awaits* and *New worlds,* Diebel's *Beckoning trails,* Russell's *Road to everywhere,* and other series of books for classroom use in Canada and the United States.

In 1941 *Jory's Cove* was produced, the first full length book written and illustrated by Clare Bice. This is the story of life in the Maritimes, of the sea, of fishing, of boats and especially of one blue sailboat that was Jamie's heart's desire.

In 1948 *Across Canada* presented eight stories with illustrations of children from various parts of our country. These are based on Dr Bice's interviews with young people in his travels from Nova Scotia to the West Coast. This title has been translated into Norwegian and is also available in braille.

A search for pirate gold along the rugged shore of Newfoundland becomes more exciting with the appearance of two strangers exploring the caves. The events of a very unusual summer are told in *The Great island* published in 1954.

An old beggar, a hungry little dog, sheep dogs trials and thieves provide plenty of action in *A Dog for Davie's Hill* published in 1957 with its setting in Scotland.

The arrival of four strangers at Ship Cove in Nova Scotia aroused suspicions and a hurricane proved helpful as mystery impeded the discovery of buried wealth in *Hurricane treasure* published in 1965.

Dr Bice has contributed to *Canadian Art* and the section on "Canadian Painting in the Twentieth Century" in *Winds of change* by Hugh Peart, and has been on the staff of the Doon School of Art, summer schools at Queen's University, Mount Allison University, University of British Columbia, and University of Western Ontario.

In 1962-63, he was awarded a Canada Council Senior Arts Fellowship and in 1962 an honorary degree of Doctor of Laws from the University of Western Ontario. He was elected academician of the Royal Canadian Academy, served as president 1967-70, and member of the Ontario Society of Artists. Dr Bice is a member of the Arts and Letters Club, Toronto and served as president of the Canadian Art Museum Directors Organization 1965-67.

Dr and Mrs Bice have one son, Kevin, who teaches Art and English in secondary school, is married with one daughter Jennie Irene. Their daughter, Megan, is in fourth year Honours History at the University of Western Ontario.

Dr Bice has contributed in many ways to Canadian education and culture. He has endeavoured to share his knowledge of art as it has been concerned with the civilization of every age and to have artistic expression considered a valid self-contained purpose. Active in many community organizations, Dr Bice has given his time and talents most generously in spite of the many demands made on him.

Londoners are proud to claim Dr Clare Bice!

Eleanore Donnelly
London Public Library and Art Museum

Hazel Boswell

Even a brief encounter with Hazel Boswell is a memorable joy. For here is a woman who has discarded the inessentials and found what is important in life. Her direct gaze and simple ease reflect an immense integrity and serenity; these inform her relations with people and make her books and water colours mirrors of dignity and charm as well.

Perhaps these attributes follow on her eighty years of just living; perhaps they naturally accrue to the descendant of five generations of Québec seigneurs. For Hazel Boswell's great-great-great-grandfather, the Marquis de Lotbinière, built Fort Ticonderoga where the French resisted the English conquest of Canada for a year. His reward was a hereditary seigneury on the south shore of the St Lawrence where Hazel Boswell spent her childhood summers and learned the stories and legends of French Canada. But it was in France and Germany and Italy where she later studied painting, and then, in Canada, water colour techniques with Horatio Walker.

She has combined these early influences in her two books. *French Canada, pictures and stories of old Quebec* was first published in 1938 and revised in 1967; *Legends of Quebec* came out in 1966.

The original illustrations for *French Canada* were exhibited in the New York Public Library in 1938 and the same autumn at the Belleville Book Fair and in some Ontario public libraries too. One Ontario city banned the book! And why? The illustration accompanying the chapter "Scotch Names" shows two men raising full glasses across a table on which sits an open liquor bottle! Later, however, several Quebec public libraries and art galleries displayed the water colours – and sets of prints were sold. The Aluminum Company of Canada bought one set for the Saguenay Inn, Arvida.

A reviewer of *French Canada* has said that only someone who knows and loves a country could make it so real and appealing to the imagination. The drawings are from life; in fact Hazel Boswell's two uncles appear in the cover illustration as young pupils at the Quebec seminary. They sit under an elm tree planted in the courtyard by the then Prince of Wales when he visited Canada in 1860. Shortly after Hazel Boswell sketched the tree lightning struck it, and it is no more – just as many of the old customs and ways she writes about are no more.

At 18 she accompanied her grandparents to British Columbia where her grandfather assumed the Lieutenant Governorship in 1900. Since then she has spent half her life in travel and living abroad. She has always returned to her old town house in Quebec City, however, and has devoted herself to work with the Labrador Educational League and to hospital work after World War I, the last few of ten years with mental patients. She volunteered for hospital work in France during that war too, but the submarine menace prevented her contingent of VAD's from sailing over.

At this writing Hazel Boswell is planning several books. She has written charming verses with accompanying drawings on childlike themes, and she has completed a world history for young people. She wrote in 1969, "I've done very little work this winter. However I managed to finish the illustrations for the MS of my mother's life, and her sister's and brother's, on the seigneurie, *Childhood on an old seigneurie*. The book is now under consideration of publication with a publisher."

A charming reminder of the artist is to receive a note written on a card which has a reproduction of one of the drawings from *Legends of Quebec* on its face – the one that illustrates this sentence from "The Little Bear:" "His mother's back was turned to their home as they drove away, but he was facing it." Such an *insouciant* little face appeals to our sympathies and recalls the story vividly.

Irma McDonough
Provincial Library Service, Toronto

7

Sheila Burnford

Conversation with Sheila Burnford, once the initial shy aloofness
has been dispelled by laughter, reveals a warm, charming person,
with a keen sense of humour, poetic insight, forthright opinions
and a disconcertingly direct gaze which suggests that she "can
see quite through the deeds of men."

Born in Scotland in 1918, and educated there and in England
and Germany, Sheila Burnford spent the early part of the
Second World War in the service of her country. Following her
marriage to Dr David Burnford, then a surgeon in the Royal
Navy, she retired from active service to attend to the rearing of
small daughters, under the watchful almond eye of an English
bullterrier named Bill. "In the long, blacked-out nights of war,
living alone in a rambling house in Sussex, I came to rely upon
him for comfort and security far more than one would in normal
times. I laugh when I look back upon it, for I used to read to
him in the evenings – excerpts from the papers and a long session
of Anthony Trollope. There was no one else to listen or to
whom I could talk, as the two oldest children were only babies,
so the terrier became my captive audience . . . . The extraordin-
ary extent of his recognition of words and phrases, far beyond
the normal range, was probably the result of those conversational
years."

Bill accompanied the Burnfords and their three daughters to Canada in 1948, when they came to live in Port Arthur, Ontario. At this point, prospective author, protagonist and landscape were juxtaposed. But more ingredients were still to be added. First of these was Simon, a Siamese kitten, acquired as companion and consolation for Bill, when the children were away all day at school: "They were closer than any other cat and dog relationship I have seen, sleeping in the same basket, hunting together, playing; and each assumed some of the other's characteristics . . . . They made a lawless pair, for the cat could open any door." Later, the doctor acquired a Labrador: ". . . always a serious law-abiding gun dog, who never participated in their kitchen raids, or joined them hunting in the woods; but as the terrier's sight began to fail him, the young dog showed the most astonishing perception and tolerance; and it became the accepted custom that he should accompany the old terrier on his morning and evening rounds of the neighbourhood garbage cans and hydrants, waiting patiently at every place of interest, steering him back on the sidewalk when he would have strayed on to the road, and finally delivering his charge home."

The stage was set, the actors in the wings – or disporting themselves over a landscape of rugged beauty – awaiting the author's inspiration. Fortunately, from the childhood environment of a book-oriented home and wide and unlimited reading, Sheila Burnford had been early imbued with the feeling that one must write. She served her apprenticeship by writing scripts for the Port Arthur Puppetry Club, which gave her scope for improvisation, the discipline of seeking motivation for a character's words and actions – and a healthy appreciation of the necessity of meeting deadlines. About the same time, she began writing articles describing the Canadian scene and way of life which found ready acceptance in *Punch* and other British periodicals. The next step was a book. With the death of the well-loved Bill at the age of 15, the book became a sort of "in memoriam" to him, as is the moving character of William in *The Fields of noon*.

"Communication between animals has always fascinated me, not just the instinctive means, but the day to day, individual and original communication that exists even between animals of diversified species when they live harmoniously with common domestic background. There were endless examples of this with our animal trio, all members of it as different in their personalities as it is possible for animals to be, yet apparently able to receive the intent or communication of the others and act upon it." From this interest, and with the desire to create a novel about animals which would have integrity and be free from mawkishness or anthropomorphism, *The Incredible journey* was born.

Sheila Burnford believes that children should be allowed to range freely in their reading. *The Incredible journey* was not written for children, but children took it to their hearts.

Translated (at last count) into 25 languages, and made into a motion picture, the saga of her three animals continues to girdle the globe, taking something of the Canadian wilderness with them, and bringing home honours to its author: in Canada, the Book of the Year medal of the Canadian Association of Children's Librarians in 1963, in the States, The William Allen White Award, the Dorothy Canfield Fisher Award, the Young People's Choice Award of the Pacific Northwestern Libraries Association, and, internationally, an honourable mention from the Hans Christian Andersen Awards Committee.

There were the customary pinpricks, of course, ranging from the critic who had decided that the author must be a "dear old lady, very furry-minded, who dotes on all four-footed animals," to the indignant letters which came on the heels of a newspaper photograph revealing that hunting was one of her hobbies. (Her others, beside writing, are mycology and astronomy.) But she had her laughter too, when she assured a Press Club gathering that she must claim the distinction of being the first author ever to share her bed with all three of her characters – at the same time!

Her next book, *The Fields of noon,* a collection of her published articles, revealed a light and deft touch, coupled with keenness of insight and warm humour. The book, a joy in itself, also holds promise of a time when this gifted and sensitive woman may turn her talent to other themes, involving the human predicament. Perhaps these books are already underway. We can only pass back to her her own admonition: "DO NOT VEGETATE!"

After dinner with me, a twinkle in her dark eyes, she gathered up the bowser bag containing the remnants of my roast lamb, which I had gladly relinquished as a peace-offering to the redoubtable Simon of 19 venerable years, who had had to stay at home that day . . . . The thought gave me pause, striking as it did a chord of recollection. But no, Tao's companions were no longer there to lure him away into the wilderness. Instead, it is his mistress who will soon be setting forth on her incredible journey.

As I write, Sheila Burnford is off on a marine biology expedition to Antarctica, in a Chilean ship, with ornithologists and other wildlife specialists, to study the birds and the sea mammals, but also, because she is a romantic person, to make a pilgrimage to the place which Captain Scott had known.

The foregoing was written in the winter of 1967-68. Now, in the summer of 1970, my path has once more briefly crossed that of Sheila Burnford, and I am once again fascinated by the wide range of her interests and her vitality.

Long before it was "fashionable" to be sympathetic to the needs and aspirations of the native peoples, Mrs Burnford was involved. Her third book, *Without reserve* published in 1969, was the product of a journal kept over a number of years during visits to the remote reserves of the Cree and Ojibwa. She and the artist, Susan Ross, sought to learn something of the language and of the life and have brought their talents together to produce this book.

Sheila Burnford and Susan Ross have now returned from a journey to the eastern Arctic, to Northern Baffin and to Bylot Island. Again a journal has been kept and sketches made. They observed the reactions of the Eskimo people to the modern invasion where "the winds of change" again propel people of the Stone Age into the twentieth century.

It is well that wise, sympathetic, and talented people record these matters, so that they are not lost in a welter of bureaucratic reports. Nevertheless, we need more books from this imaginative pen, and to accomplish that, perhaps these world wandering feet must pause a while.

A little footnote belongs here concerning another wanderer. At 20, full of years and honours, Simon (Tao) has rejoined his companions of *The Incredible journey*. The trio are reunited, as they will always be in the recollection of readers the world over.

Dorothy M. Reid
Thunder Bay Public Library

George Clutesi

"Have you ever seen an Indian?" An audience of children and adults were asked this question at a "Family Night" program in a public library. The guest speaker, author-illustrator George Clutesi, gained the close attention of his audience with this intriguing opening remark, and proceeded to recount his experiences as an Indian. He is a member of the west coast Nootka tribe whose people live on a 700 acre Tse-Shaht reserve near Port Alberni, British Columbia. In warm and moving tones, Mr Clutesi recalled his father's teaching that all people should be treated equally. This philosophy sparked his own determination to preserve the values of his native culture inherent in these words of his father, "My son, when a man passes in his canoe, if you are too poor to offer him bread, call him in anyway to rest, and to share the warmth of your fire."

At a time when the white man is observing and analyzing the plight of the Canadian Indian in our society, George Clutesi turns a mildly critical gaze on the white man's world which he says is producing "stereotyped non-humans." A literate and articulate spokesman for the Indian, Mr Clutesi favours a positive non-militant approach to focusing attention on their problems. In his various roles as artist, writer, lecturer, folklorist and guest on radio and television, he has become a significant voice for his people.

Mr Clutesi, a protégé of Emily Carr, gained recognition first as an artist. His large 40 foot mural depicting a wolf and a killer whale covered an entire wall of the Indian pavilion at Expo in Montreal. More recently, he has been invited to hold a one man show at the Banff Museum and Archives of the Canadian Rockies.

His first book *Son of Raven, Son of Deer* was published in 1967. It has been accepted in British Columbia schools as an elementary English text and has also been included in an English Course at the University of British Columbia. This is surely a tribute to the author and his publisher, Gray's Publishing Ltd of Sidney, B.C. *Son of Raven, Son of Deer* is a collection of 12 fables based on ancient stories told to him by his father, the last of a long line of story-tellers who for over four hundred years preserved a rich heritage of oral literature. His illustrations for the book show him to be an accomplished craftsman in both arts.

His second book, *Potlatch,* has been compared to the novels of Joseph Conrad. It describes the most important winter festival of the west coast Indians and provides the reader with a unique introduction to Indian culture through the author's eye-witness account of the ceremonies which were outlawed by the government for many years. Mr Clutesi is currently writing *Stand tall my son,* which describes the whale hunts of the Tse-Shaht people.

Clutesi has not achieved recognition in his chosen art forms without hardship and struggle. He was a pile-driver for 21 of his 66 years, but he suffered a broken back and turned to painting during his convalescence. It is not surprising that he is also a poet. His prose has a lyrical quality that is equally apparent in his writing and speaking. Interviewed on the Canadian Broadcasting Company's *Front Page Challenge,* he said he is grateful that Canadian Indians are questioning the Federal Government's plans for them. "The reserve," he says, "is our last link with the soil we've loved so much."

He added, "I try not to harbour resentment." He wants to forget that in 1967 he was not even invited to attend the unveiling of his mural at Expo, and that he and other Indian artists were treated with indifference and discourtesy by government officials. By 1969, policies in the Indian Affairs Department had changed, and on a trip to Ottawa, Montreal and Toronto, Mr Clutesi was received with courtesy and consideration.

Mr Clutesi speaks proudly of his three sons and three daughters and of his hopes for their future. In *Potlatch,* he describes the heir apparent of the Tse-Shaht people.
"He was a big man. An imposing man.
His limbs were lithe, lean and strong.
There was pride in the way he moved.
Slow and lazy, like the stream that runs deep.
There was no room for arrogance in his face."
This epilogue might very well describe the author.

Elaine de Temple
Ottawa Public Library

Lyn Cook

Lyn Cook is a name well known to Canadian children, librarians, parents, teachers – to anyone in fact involved with children and books. She has written ten books for children and is a leading figure in the field of children's creative drama. She is a warm, vital person with a lively interest in the world around her and a special feeling for children.

Lyn was born 4 May 1918 near Weston and her first school years were spent in a small two room country school. The Cooks moved to Mount Dennis and then to Islington where she won a scholarship to the University of Toronto. She graduated in English language and literature in 1940, and attended library school the next year.

After one year on the staff of the Toronto Public Library she joined the RCAF-WD. She was in the Meteorological Service for three years, but spent her last year in the service organizing a library at Trenton for the men who were being demobilized. (One of her volunteer poster artists was Phil Aziz, now a well-known painter in London, Ontario.)

After the war Lyn joined the staff of the Sudbury Public Library as their first children's librarian. Here she wrote her first book for children, *Bells on Finland Street*. It is about a Finnish-Canadian Sudbury girl who wants to be a world champion figure skater. This best known of her books continues as the best loved. It has been translated into German and is now published in Switzerland.

In the library she introduced creative drama; children acted out the stories she told. From this beginning in creative drama sprang a radio program, *Doorway in Fairyland,* broadcast over CKSO Sudbury. It was so well received that the Canadian Broadcasting Corporation requested the program and Lyn come to Toronto to take up a new career in radio.

Shortly after this she married Robb Waddell whom she had met in the RCAF. Marriage did not interfere with her radio work however, and her program continued to be broadcast on the trans-Canada network of the CBC and over seven American stations.

Successful and time-consuming though her radio show was Lyn continued to write for publication. *The Little magic fiddler* appeared in 1951. It is the story of Donna Grescoe, the young Winnipeg girl who became famous as a child violinist. Donna's Ukrainian background lends colour to the story of her struggle to achieve her goal.

Doorway in Fairyland was now in its fifth year and though its popularity showed no signs of waning Lyn moved out of broadcasting to raise a family. Her first child, a boy, was born in 1952. A daughter arrived the next year.

These were busy years for the new mother but Lyn still found time to write *Rebel on the trail* which made its appearance in 1953. It has a pioneer backwoods setting somewhere near Milton, and relates the involvement of a family, particularly the children, in the 1837 Rebellion. The young heroine is named Deborah, as is Lyn's daughter.

Shortly after the publication of this book Lyn began writing scripts for another radio show, *Sounds Fun*. At the same time she contributed plots for *Uncle Chichimus,* a puppet show produced by John Conway. And a fourth book was published in 1955, a boy's story this time. *Jady and the General* tells of a farm boy's longing for a horse and involves competition at the Royal Winter Fair in Toronto.

Two years later *Pegeen and the pilgrim,* a regional story set in Stratford, Ontario appeared. A 12 year old girl and a boarding house participate in the Stratford Shakespearean Festival!

Meanwhile Lyn began to teach creative play making in the New Play Society Drama School which was founded and developed by Dora Mavor Moore. Her association with the New Play Society continued for nearly ten years, and during this time she published *The Road to Kip's Cove* in 1961. This story of friendship between a white boy and an Indian boy takes the reader on an exciting canoe trip down the Trent Canal during an adventurous summer holiday. The central figure is named for Lyn's own son, Christopher.

The Waddells make their home in Scarborough and almost inevitably Lyn found herself doing extension work in story-telling and creative drama at her local library, the Bendale branch. She speaks about her books and writing as a career to teachers and children whenever she is invited to do so. And she continues writing. *Samantha's secret room* appeared in 1963. Samantha's search for a secret room in her family's farm overlooking Penetang Bay provides an exciting touch of mystery to this regional story. The *Brownie handbook* came out two years later and it is known and loved by some 100,000 Canadian Brownies.

Lyn's ninth book for children and her second historical novel was published in 1966. A secret friendship between Henrietta, daughter of a wealthy Napanee citizen, and a little lost waif forms the basis of the plot of *The Secret of Willow Castle*. Woven through this story of Upper Canada in 1834 is Henrietta's close bond with her cousin, John A. Macdonald. This book has an authentic background; the girl is real, and the house still stands on the banks of the Napanee River.

In view of her varied careers it is no surpise that Lyn Cook is in television too. She has made many television appearances, but she has also adapted *Samantha's secret room* for a national school telecast. A series of telecasts during Centennial year was based on *Pegeen and the pilgrim,* updated to 1967, and shown on the national network of the CBC-TV. *The Magical Miss Mittens* appeared in 1970. It is a regional fantasy that takes place in a Nova Scotia village, and three children have fun being travellers in time.

Whatever else she may be doing and however widespread her activities Lyn Cook is first and foremost a writer. To her, writing is as natural and essential as breathing, and there is no doubt that young readers may look forward to many more stories by a favourite author.

Ruth Maydan

Monique Corriveau

Monique Corriveau ne manque pas d'entrain, de vivacité et d'humour. Tout, autour d'elle, semble lui communiquer la joie de vivre. Elle est aussi parfaitement à l'aise à une réunion d'éditeurs et d'écrivains que sous une tente érigée en plein bois. Amoureuse de l'espace et du grand air, elle passe l'été à la campagne, aux Eboulements, où, sans doute, elle a tiré un bon nombre de mises en scène de ses romans. Il faut être un peu magicienne pour être à la fois, la maman de dix enfants, dont l'âge varie de 16 à 3 ans et ècrivain aussi prolifique. Prolifique? Elle me confie que c'est grâce à ses enfants. Parce qu'elle a dédié son premier roman à Matthieu, son fils aîné, les autres enfants réclament le leur. Donc, il n'est plus possible de faire marche arrière après s'être compromise de telle façon et il lui faudra écrire au moins dix romans. Soyez assurée, chère madame, que nous serons les derniers à nous en plaindre. Parfaite hôtesse et cordon-bleu, elle ouvre sa maison toute grande à tous les amis.

"Ecrire, c'est facile," dit-elle, "s'agit de s'y mettre." Elle s'étonne qu'un si petit nombre de canadiens-français s'adonnent à cet art qui, pour elle, est un métier passionnant. Elle souhaite   17 que plus d'écrivains se consacrent à la littérature enfantine canadienne et suggère que nous nous mettions à la tâche. "Vous verrez, ça vient tout seul," affirme-t-elle. Avis aux intéressés!

Née d'une famille aux goûts littéraires, elles commença très jeune à composer des romans, qu'elle a d'ailleurs conservés dans une caisse, où elle va encore piger pour bâtir les intrigues de ses romans, maintenant devenus une réalité. Toujours secondée dans ses efforts par tous les membres de sa famille: son père, qui lui-même maniait fort bien la plume, une vieille cousine, qui écrivait sous le pseudonyme de Maxine, que les enfants connaissent bien, sa soeur Suzanne Martel, qui est elle-même écrivain bien connu, son mari et ses enfants, qui lui fournissent les personnages et le décor gratuitement, Monique Corriveau a doté la littérature enfantine canadienne, depuis les dernières dix années, de charmants récits d'aventures et d'intrigues policières que les enfants adorent.

Il est évident que l'auteur de *Les jardiniers du hibou*, *Le secret de Vanille*, *Messire* et *La petite fille du printemps* est la grande amie des enfants, qu'elle les connaît parfaitement et qu'elle les adore. Elle sait la dose exacte de tous les ingrédients nécessaires pour nouer et dénouer une intrigue policière. Tous ses petits détectives en herbe se tirent toujours assez bien d'affaire et, un fait à noter, presque toujours en l'absence des parents. "Une histoire conçue pour les enfants doit se dérouler autour des enfants eux-mêmes, avec un minimum de personnages adultes" explique-t-elle.

La série *Max*, dont les deux premiers volumes seulement ont été publiés, nous réserve d'agréables surprises. Une des histoires renferme d'intèressantes péripéties à bord d'un planeur, et se passe en partie dans l'ouest du Canada. Elle se documenta lors d'un voyage à Calgary, en 1966 où l'Association Canadienne des Bibliothécaires de l'Enfants lui remettait la médaille de bronze décernée au meilleur roman pour enfants et attribuée, cette année-là, à son roman intitulé *Le Wapiti*. Un autre *Max* aurait pour décor, la fascinante Ile du Prince Edouard, où l'auteur a passé un été enchanteur avec sa famille. Un troisième *Max* renfermerait quelques scènes d'un certain concert sous les étoiles au Camp Fortune dans la vallée de La Gatineau. Et voici comment Monique Corriveau cueille à pleines mains, à même la vie de tous les jours, ces innombrables incidents qui ravissent les enfants.

Le Wapiti, cependant, demeure son roman préféré, avoue-t-elle. Serait-ce parce qu'il compte parmi les premiers de sa carrière? Depuis sa publication, il a été traduit en anglais. Il lui a mérité la médaille de l'Association Canadienne des Bibliothécaires pour Enfants. L'intrigue de ce roman est quelque peu différente des autres puisqu'il s'agit ici de l'histoire d'un jeune Français recueilli par des Indiens, après qu'il ait dû refugier dans la forêt, après un meurtre, dont il a été accusé à tort. La trame du récit se déroule aussi en plein vieux Québec, au tout début de la colonie.

Monique Corriveau, tous les enfants du pays vous saluent et vous rendent hommage! Ils envient vos petits qui ont, à leur service, une maman qui peut sur demande et en un tournemain, leur fabriquer une belle histoire qui leur est dédiée, tout en faisant dorer une tarte aux framboises. Bravo Monique! Les enfants attendent vos *Max* avec impatience.

Et Monique Corriveau a tenu sa promesse en nous donnant en 1968 *Cécile, Trois contes pour enfants,* après *Max au rallye,* toujours chez les Editions Jeunesse. Ses contes ont remporté le prix du Centenaire de la Confédération. Une édition scolaire de *Les jardiniers du hibou* avec fiches de travail pour les 5e et 6e annees de même que des fiches pour *Le secret de Vanille* sont parues à l'Education Nouvelle, à Montréal. M. Klinck a adapté *Max* et *Max au rallye* pour l'enseignement du français aux étudiants de langue anglaise avec lexique et questionnaires.

Depuis longtemps Monique Corriveau désirait écrire un roman pour adultes. Son rêve devint réalité lorsqu'en 1969, le Cercle du Livre de France publia *Le témoin,* qui connaît déjà beaucoup de succès.

Agathe Dicaire
Conseillère en Services de Bibliothèques Scolaires
Ministère de l'Education d'Ontario

Monique Corriveau is endowed with high spirits, vivacity, humour and exudes the joy of living. She is as perfectly at ease with editors and writers as she is in a tent pitched in the woods. A lover of the wide open spaces, and fresh air, she spends the summer in the country at Eboulements which has, no doubt, provided much of the material for her novels. One has to be something of a magician to be both mother of ten children whose ages range from 3 to 16 and also a prolific writer. She confided to me that she owed this to her family. Because she dedicated her first novel to Matthieu, her eldest son, the other children expect the same, so it is impossible to stop until she has written at least ten novels! Her readers will be the last to complain. Perfect hostess and excellent cook, her house is always wide open to her many friends.

She says that "writing is easy, it's just a matter of going ahead with it." She is amazed that so very few French Canadians take up the art which, to her, is fascinating. She wishes that more writers would devote themselves to Canadian children's literature and suggests that we should explore this field. "You will see that it comes automatically," she says.

Born to a literary family, she started quite young to compose stories and often draws on this cache of early material to build up the plots for her novels. Always encouraged in her efforts by all the members of the family: her father, himself a master with the pen, an old cousin who wrote under the pseudonym of Maxime, and whom the children know very well, her sister Suzanne Martel, who is also a well-known writer, her husband and her children, Mrs Corriveau has been adding charming adventure and detective stories to Canadian children's literature for the last ten years, and the children love them.

19

It is obvious that the author of *Les jardiniers du hibou, Le secret de Vanille, Messire* and *La petite fille du printemps* is a great friend to children, knows them perfectly and adores them. She knows the exact measure of all the ingredients needed to knit and unravel a detective plot. All her budding young detectives manage to extricate themselves creditably from tight situations, almost invariably in the absence of their parents. "A story conceived for children," she says, "should unfold around children, with a minimum of adult characters."

The *Max* series, of which only the first two books have been published, has some pleasant surprises in store for us. One of the plots contains interesting incidents aboard a glider and takes place partly in western Canada. She gathered material for this story during a trip to Calgary in 1966 when she was presented with the Canadian Association of Children's Librarians Book of the Year for Children medal for the best children's novel, given that year for her novel, *The Wapiti*. Another *Max* has Prince Edward Island as a setting, where the author spent a golden summer with her family. A third *Max* contains some scenes from an open-air concert at Camp Fortune in the Gatineau Valley. Monique Corriveau gathers the numerous incidents that entrance children so much from her everyday life.

She admits, however, that *The Wapiti* is still her favourite novel. Perhaps because it is among the first ones of her career? Since its publication it has been translated into English. The plot of this prize-winning novel is somewhat different from the others being the story of a French boy who is given shelter by the Indians when he has to flee to the forest after he is wrongfully accused of murder. The story unfolds in old Quebec at its very beginning as a colony.

Canadian children must envy Monique Corriveau's family whose mother can concoct wonderful stories in a twinkling and dedicate them to her children. They are waiting impatiently for more of *Max*.

Since 1968, Monique Corriveau has published with Editions Jeunesse, *Cécile, Three short stories for children*, which won the award Centenaire de la Confédération. *Les jardiniers du hibou* and *Le secret de Vanille* appeared in a school edition at Education Nouvelle with study guides for grades five and six. M. Klinck has adapted *Max* and *Max au rallye* for the teaching of French to English-speaking students, adding glossaries, notes and study guides.

Monique Corriveau finally realized her secret ambition when she published *Le témoin* her first novel for adults. It appeared at Le Cercle du Livre de France in 1969 and has rapidly become a best-seller.

20

John Craig

Long ago when summer lasted forever my mother used to take my brother and me on excursions in the good ship *Stoney Lake*. They were not so hilarious as that well-known episode of the *Mariposa Belle*, but they were full of excitement and adventure. Those lake steamers fondly remembered by many who cottaged on the Kawartha and Muskoka Lakes might seem ponderous tubs to modern youngsters, but what joy they brought. Remember those days? Bless my soul, I do. And so does John Craig.

Remember the fun of playing Indian? Remember the canoe that came at least once a summer with baskets and fish, paddled by tall dark mysterious Indians whose prowess with a paddle filled your heart with envy? John Craig remembers, and I'll bet he can paddle like that.

Just before I met John Craig I read *By the sound of her whistle* and realized that he was a writer from home. He was born in Peterborough on 2 July 1921, and I must confess we spent most of our meeting remembering the good old days in Peterborough when Youngs of Young's Point ran the *Islinda* and the other lake boats, when PCVS had the greatest rugby team in the province – just about!

John Craig seems always to have had many interests, many irons in the fire. For example, one winter he belonged to three basketball teams each of which won in their separate leagues, and the three final games were played in Port Hope, Peterborough and Port Perry within 24 hours and the last game was won 104 to 6. I believe his devotion to basketball that year was greater than his devotion to school. After the war he went to the so-called "school of the quick and the dead" doing four years of high school study in eight months. At the University of Manitoba he won the first William Lyon Mackenzie King Fellowship, and received his MA from Toronto.

The first of his books that I read was *The Long return* (1959). That it is out of print seems too bad for it is a good yarn about a white boy stolen away by Indians. The plot and character development are fine and compelling. (There are too few good Canadian "juveniles" to let them go OP without some word of protest. This is mine.)

Then I read *No word for goodbye* (1969) and thought that this is the sort of book we need, right now, right here. It speaks to our young and compels them to recognize the unjustness of a society that could set up and maintain the reservation policy with all its implications. "Everybody is equal before the law – but with all their lawyers, they were just a little more equal than we were, I guess" . . . "Maybe they could appeal" . . . "The Ojibway are proud, they're gone from here for good."

By the sound of her whistle (1966) is affectionate reminiscing about the Youngs, how they got to Clear Lake and how they became involved in steam boating on the Kawarthas. It is a book to charm more than the Peterborough County old timers for here is a true pioneering tale of staunch men who helped make this country.

In *The Pro* (1968) Mr Craig has written a powerful novel about National League hockey. The climax is a rebellion against management for an unjust suspension, and as in all of his books there is no contrived happy ending.

Mr Craig is strong enough to say "I work in order to have money to write," and mean it. But there's more to it than that. There's his sense of rebellion against injustice – to the laws that confine Canadian Indians to a poverty level existence on their reserves, against management when it is unfair. He is a crusader, in fact.

His style improves with every book, and his books are honest, well written, a pleasure to have in the library. He was a consultant for the new television series *Rainbow Country,* that carries on the crusade he's involved in: the fight for the rights of our red brothers.

Elizabeth C. English
Thunder Bay Public Library

Paule Daveluy

Paule Cloutier est née à Ville-Marie, Québec, chef-lieu du comté de Témiscamingue, le 6 Avril 1919. Ainée d'une famille de cinq enfants, elle habite la Métropole depuis l'âge de trois ans. Elle fit ses études, cours primaire et cours Lettres-Sciences, au Pensionnat Mont-Royal. Elle poursuivit deux années de cours de service social chez les Soeurs du Bon-Conseil. Elle a obtenu le poste de secrétaire à CKAC, où très tôt on lui confia la redaction d'émissions radiophoniques.

En 1944, elle épousa André Daveluy, son patron; six enfants naquirent de cette heureuse union.

Les Daveluy habitent Cartierville, en banlieue de Montréal, où Monsieur est marguillier de la paroisse Sainte-Odile et où Madame Daveluy traduit des albums à colorier et sert de secrétaire à son mari, "Monsieur Bricole" de la Patrie, de CKLM et de CJAD.

Elle a collaboré a plusieurs périodiques locaux: *Notre Temps, Hérauts, La Famille, 20e siècle, Mieux,* etc. Pour la radio, elle a donné des textes monologués quotidiens: *Le Journal de Pierre*

Clément (avec Michel Noël) *Passetemps de Femmes* (avec Emile Genest), *Le Baluchon aux Epices* (avec Mario Verdon), et, pendant cinq ans, *Sans Tambour ni Trompette*. Elle a gagné un des prix littéraires offert par les Editions Fides pour une nouvelle, *Conciergerie* (1950), publiée dans le volume *Trois nouvelles*. Elle a fait paraître, aux Editions de l'Atelier, un recueil d'anecdotes sous le titre, *Les Guinois* (1957). Ce sont, comme l'indique le sous-titre, des "Chroniques de la maison heureuse." (Heurs et malheurs des parents, de la mère surtout, d'une petite famille grandissante aux prises avec les réalités quotidiennes). Puis ce fut un roman psychologique pour adultes, *Chérie Martin*.

L'été enchanté (1958), ce fut le premier livre du cycle des saisons, gagnat la médaille de bronze de l'Association Canadienne des Bibliothécaires pour Enfants, puisqu'il fut le meilleur livre français pour la jeunesse. Traduit et édité aux Etats-Unis, et mentionné par le journal *Time* comme l'un des cent meilleurs livres pour la jeunesse publiés aux Etats-Unis en 1962, *Summer in Ville-Marie* a été édité aussi en Angleterre, en 1963, et ré-édité aux Editions Jeunesse en 1963. Il a été choisi comme livre du base accompagnant le manuel de français des F.S.C., septième année, en 1964. *Drôle d'automne* (1962), fut le deuxième livre du cycle des saisons. L'auteur a gagné le Prix du Salon du Livre de Québec, en 1962, ainsi que la médaille de l'ACBE (première auteur à obtenir deux fois la médaille.) Choisi par le Département de l'Instruction Publique comme lecture obligatoire dans les classes de dixième (filles), à travers la Province de Québec, ce livre fut ré-édité aux Editions Jeunesse.

Vinrent ensuite *Sylvette et les adultes* (1962), mention de l'ACELF à son concours littéraire, *Sylvette sous la tente bleue, Cinq filles compliquées* et le troisième livre du cycle des saisons *Cet hiver-là* (1967). Les nombreux lecteurs attendent impatiemment la parution du quatrième livre du cycle des saisons, *Cher printemps*.

Dans ses romans, Mme Daveluy n'essaie pas de refaire la vie, mais essaie d'en dégager un sain réalisme. Ceux-ci sont des romans d'amour bien racontés, qui n'ont rien d'emprunté, d'exagéré ou de sophistiqué pour les adolescents. Mme Daveluy connaît bien l'âme des adolescents; ses livres le prouvent abondamment: justes sur le plan psychologique et impeccables sur le plan formel. Ses récits sont racontés d'un ton optimiste avec cet humour délicat qui caractérise le style de cet écrivain.

La pensée de l'auteur

"Il est naturel que j'aie voulu écrire pour les adolescents, ma jeunesse me semble encore si proche, à regarder grandir mes filles. Mais il faudra chaque fois, relever le défi: faire intéressant, captivant, sans troubler les coeurs neufs, sans ternir les yeux clairs. Les jeunes lisent tellement de livres qui expliquent, racontent, exaltent les décors, les faits d'armes, l'âme français que canadiens; il est temps qu'on rétablisse la situation. Forte de cette conviction, je m'emploie à écrire des livres qui parlent un français international."

Madame Daveluy, les adolescents du Canada vous sont reconnaissants parce que vous avez su leur faire comprendre, par vos écrits, comment accepter les peines et les joies de la vie, telles qu'elles existent, et non comme dans un conte de fée. Tous attendent avec impatience *Cher printemps*. A quand la bonne nouvelle?

Marguerite Polnicky
Leon XIII Separate School Library, Sudbury

Paule Cloutier was born in Ville-Marie, Quebec, county town of Témiscamingue, on 6 April 1919. Eldest of a family of five, she has lived in Montreal from the age of three. Educated at Mount Royal School for Girls, she subsequently took two years of a social service course with the Soeurs du Bon Conseil. She obtained a position as secretary at radio station CKAC where very soon she was put in charge of editing radio broadcasts.

In 1944 Paule Cloutier married her director, André Daveluy and there are six children of this happy marriage. The Daveluys live in Cartierville in the suburbs of Montreal where he is churchwarden of St Odile parish church. There Mrs Daveluy translates colouring books and acts as secretary to her husband, "Monsieur Bricole" de la Patrie, of radio and television stations CKLM and CJAD. Mr Daveluy is also the author of the *Do it yourself encyclopaedia* published in French.

Mrs Daveluy has collaborated on several local periodicals, *Notre Temps* (Our Times), *Hérauts* (The Heralds), *La Famille* (The Family), *20e Siècle* (Twentieth Century) *Mieux* (Better), etc. For radio she has supplied the scripts for the daily programs, *Le Journal de Pierre Clément* (Pierre Clément's Dairy), with Michel Noel; *Passetemps de Femmes* (Women's Pastimes) with Emile Genest; *Le Baluchon aux Epices* (The Spice Box) with Mario Verdon; and for the last five years, *Sans Tambour ni Trompette* (Without Drum or Trumpet). She won a literary prize given by Editions Fides for a short story *Conciergerie* (Caretaker's Lodge) (1950) included in the book *Trois Nouvelles* (Three Novellas). Through Editions de l'Atelier she has published a collection of short stories under the title *Les Guinois* (1957). These were, as the sub-title indicates, "stories of the happy home," about the fortunes and misfortunes of family life, mostly about the mother of a small family growing up in the grip of the realities of day to day life. Then there was a psychological novel for adults, *Chérie Martin* (Dear Martin).

L'été enchanté (The Enchanted Summer) 1958, the first book of a cycle of the seasons, in 1960 won the bronze medal of the Canadian Association of Children's Librarians for the best children's book in French. Translated and published in the United States and mentioned in *Time* as one of the hundred best books for children published in the U.S. in 1962, *Summer in Ville Marie* was also published in England in 1963 and republished by Editions Jeunesse in 1963. It was chosen as the source book to accompany the French handbook of the F.S.C. for the seventh grade in 1964. *Drôle d'automne* (Strange

25

Autumn) 1962 is the second book of the cycle of the seasons. For it the author won the Salon du livre de Québec prize in 1962, as well as the CACL medal (the first author to win the medal twice). Chosen by the Department of Education as compulsory reading in grade ten for girls for the whole of the province in Quebec, this book was re-printed by Editions Jeunesse. There followed *Sylvette et les adultes* (Sylvette and the Grown-ups) (1962) which received honourable mention from ACELF at its book fair; *Sylvette sous la tente bleue* (Sylvette in the blue tent), *Cinq filles compliquées* (Five complicated girls) and the third book of the cycle of the seasons *Cet Hiver-là* (Last Winter) (1967). Many readers are impatiently awaiting the publication of the fourth book in the cycle, *Cher printemps* (Sweet spring). Les Editions Jeunesse will publish her translation of *With pipe, paddle and song* by Elizabeth Yates in the spring of 1971. In her novels, Mrs Daveluy does not try to remake life but attempts to abstract from it a healthy reality. They are novels of love, well-told, which are not far-fetched, exaggerated or too sophisticated for young people. Mrs Daveluy understands young people's feelings; her books prove it abundantly. They are psychologically sound and formally impeccable. These stories have an optimistic cast and a delicate humour which characterize this author's style.

The author's thought
"It is natural that I want to write for young people; my youth still seems so close, as I watch my girls growing up. But one must always keep in mind the challenge: make it interesting, captivating without troubling young hearts, without clouding clear eyes. Young people read so many books which explain, recount and play up the background of war and the French spirit that they become much more French than Canadian in spirit; it is time to remedy this situation. Strengthened by this conviction I occupy myself by writing books which speak a French for all people."

Mrs Daveluy, the young people of Canada are grateful to you because you have made them understand, through your writings, how to accept the troubles and joys of life, as they exist and not as they are in a fairy tale. We all wait impatiently for *Cher printemps*. When shall we hear the good news?

Cliff Faulknor

Clifford Vernon Faulknor, a Westerner by birth and by choice, was born in Vancouver, British Columbia in 1913. He graduated from high school in 1929, and during the depression years that preceded the outbreak of World War II, he worked for a time in a bank, and later in the lumber industry. His fondness for outdoor life led young Faulknor to apply for a position with the British Columbia Forest Service, and he eventually became an assistant ranger.

During the war, Mr Faulknor served with the Canadian Army as a marine diesel engineer on a transport vessel. After his discharge from the army, he studied at the University of British Columbia in the Faculty of Agriculture, majoring in Plant Science. In 1949 he obtained his Bachelor of Science degree, graduating with first class honours.

Mr Faulknor was for several years a land inspector for the British Columbia Department of Lands and Forests. Having been keenly interested in writing since high school days, he began sending articles and stories to newspapers in Vancouver and Victoria. For more than a year *Victoria Times* published his articles in a weekly column.

In 1954 Cliff Faulknor took a position in Winnipeg with the *Country Guide,* a national farm monthly magazine. A year later he became the firm's Western Field Editor, and at present he is Associate Editor with headquarters in Calgary, Alberta.

In his leisure time he writes nonfiction articles, fiction, and boys' adventure stories, many of which have been published in magazines in Canada, Great Britain and the United States.

The White calf, Mr Faulknor's first full-length novel for boys, won the third Little, Brown Children's Book Award in 1965. This award is given to an unpublished children's book manuscript judged by the joint editorial boards of the Canadian and American divisions of Little, Brown to be the best submitted by a Canadian author. *The White calf* is a moving story about a Piegan Blackfoot boy growing up and learning to take his place among the men of the tribe. It is convincingly and simply told against a background rich in authentic Indian lore. The author's empathy with the Prairie Indian and his talent for graphic description make *The White calf* a story that boys will remember. In 1966, *The White peril,* a sequel to *The White calf,* appeared. It was reviewed in the Winter, 1967 issue of *In Review.*

Both books are illustrated with superb line drawings by an Alberta artist, Gerald Tailfeathers. The artist's first tutor was his uncle who had painted on skins. Later he received art instruction in Montana and at the Banff School of Fine Arts. After working as a commercial artist in two Alberta cities for a time, Gerald Tailfeathers decided to return to the Blood Indian Reserve near Fort Macleod, Alberta. The Glenbow Foundation has a number of his paintings and sketches and many others are privately owned. Recently Gerald Tailfeathers was honoured by receiving a commission to paint a mural for the Indian exhibit at Expo '67.

A third book by Cliff Faulknor, entitled *The In-betweener* was released for sale in the spring of 1967. His fourth, another adventure story of the Piegan Blackfoot Indians, *The Smoke horse* was published in 1968.

Grace McDonald
Edmonton Public Library

Dorothy
Jane Goulding

The committee members looked worried. "Miss Goulding has promised to produce a Christmas play for us but she is still at the farm and it's nearly the end of October." The chairman told us not to worry – if Miss Goulding said she would do something, it would be done. We had no idea what had been happening at the farm during the summer but by the beginning of December the music was all arranged, the masque written and in just two full rehearsals an original production was created, not in the church hall but right in the chancel of the church – a much more difficult task. Two of the Stratford company helped with the production, one acting as narrator, and a cutter from the Festival wardrobe department produced wonderful costumes from the most improbable raw materials. The children will long remember the thrill of being made up for the performance by William Needles, and the stimulating experience of being directed by his wife.

29

Dorothy Jane Goulding plays many roles. Mother of five children ranging in age from 13 to 23, she finds time to be an author, playwright, editor for the CBC and drama consultant, and to look after a house in Toronto, a hundred acre farm and three dogs. The farm is near enough to the city that the family can live there all summer and keep in touch with their many interests. The boys built a barn last summer and Arthur bought a set of drums a few years ago from the proceeds of his "pig-keeping" summer. Jane, the elder daughter, is away from home now, acting as company manager for a cross-Canada tour of Les Jeunes Comédiens, an offshoot of the Théâtre du Nouveau Monde of Montreal. Laura, the youngest member of the family, is very domesticated and a constant help in her mother's busy life. Reid, now 16, enjoyed a great success when he toured with a production of *Dandy Lion* several years ago.

Miss Goulding's first two books, *Dorothy Jane's book* and *Dorothy Jane's other book* were published in connection with her CBC program, *Kindergarten of the Air,* which she conducted for nine years. Many mothers have reason to be grateful to her for keeping their children so well occupied at coffee break time on weekday mornings! One of her most interesting assignments was to edit *A Guide for school lighting* for the American Society of Illuminating Engineers. The task of putting the engineering jargon into clear and concise English was not easy, as anyone who has tried to cope with a technical publication will appreciate. In her work as editor for the CBC Canadian Short Stories programs, Miss Goulding has a unique opportunity to assess modern Canadian writing. She sifts through thousands of stories to find the few eventually produced on the program, for the writers are prolific, often sending in 15 when one is requested! They seem to follow a pattern – murders in January and February, boy and dog in spring, the lovable tramp in summer and the perennial moose in fall.

In *Margaret,* her story of an Irish immigrant girl who came to Canada in the eighteenth century, Miss Goulding has succeeded in making history live for young people. This exciting book shows a tremendous attention to correct historical detail, since the author uses all the library facilities at her disposal, sparing no effort to make the background authentic.

The text for Boris Spremo's beautiful book, *Toronto,* was written by Miss Goulding. She is well qualified to write on the subject, for her mother's family, the Masseys, made possible the erection of many of the city's public buildings, and were among Toronto's earliest residents. Hart House, Massey Hall and the new Massey College all testify to their public-spirited generosity. It is not surprising that Miss Goulding is so interested in drama – her mother, Dorothy Goulding, was well known in another generation for her long association with the Toronto Children's Players and William Needles, her husband, is a stalwart of the Canadian theatre, having been a member of the Stratford company for eleven seasons and a well-known theatrical figure in all parts of Canada. His work frequently takes him away from home, yet there is a quality of permanence and serenity in their home life which is too rarely seen in theatrical circles.

Tinder box, written and produced by Dorothy Jane Goulding, toured all of southern and northern Ontario making it possible for over 170,000 children to see a theatrical production – many for the first time. Another even more ambitious project will be a bilingual production of her play, *The Master cat,* which she hopes will tour Ontario next year. Miss Goulding feels that the theatre provides an ideal form of education for children and prefers live productions to films since they give a superior feeling of inter-communication. In her work as drama consultant with the Etobicoke Board of Education she has an opportunity to advise schools in the many uses of drama in the classroom and to give courses for drama teachers. Her latest book, *We're doing a play,* is a collection of short plays with a minimum of dialogue, designed for young children who are not able to read sufficiently to memorize lines. Published in 1969, it will provide material for teachers of creative drama.

One senses an irresistible creative force in Dorothy Jane Goulding. She is fortunate in having the energy and imagination to carry out her multitude of ideas.

Barbara Smiley
Provincial Library Service, Toronto

Richard Harrington

Lyn Harrington

Lyn Harrington has taken more opportunities than the rest of us to travel in Canada and abroad. Her husband Richard is a travel photographer who earns his living illustrating books and articles about Canada and foreign countries. Their working partnership provides a degree of independent travel. Together they have gone on "working visits" to over sixty countries. On her own Mrs Harrington continues to search for original material and writes about her travels and experiences.

After several years of criss-crossing Canada the Harringtons decided to see the rest of the world – "to see Canada from the outside." Their first trip was around the world – Hawaii, Fiji, New Zealand, Australia, Mauritius and Egypt; next came Africa; then the British Isles and Scandinavia; Greece, Turkey and Portugal; and in 1965 three months in Communist China.

Lyn Harrington was born Evelyn Davis on 31 July 1911 of a Sault Ste Marie family of ordinary means. After graduation from the Sault Collegiate Institute, she worked in the public library, and then took the diploma course at the University of Toronto Library School. She returned to the library as the children's librarian, a position she held for 15 years. Under her direction the children's library was extended and improved. Her story hours and puppet shows brought a great many children to the library where there was a varied and well selected book collection. Closer liaison was established with the schools, and books were made more easily available to children living some distance from the main library.

Her marriage to Richard Harrington in 1942 ended her association with the library. They moved to Toronto and from this base into the wider world.

It is a commonplace to suggest that Lyn Harrington's work as a children's librarian fostered her interest in children's literature, and especially Canadian children's literature. In her new role as a free lance writer she became very concerned about the work and welfare of Canadian authors. She joined the Toronto Branch of the Canadian Authors Association, and when she was president there was an added interest in the meetings and discussions. She is presently National Secretary of the Association and its representative on the Board of Governors of the Canadian Copyright Institute. Mrs Harrington has strong feelings about the poor rewards that come to Canadian authors. She is leading a battle to have some form of remuneration to authors for books circulated by libraries.

Lyn Harrington's works are based on Canadian and foreign subjects. About her Canadian travels and experiences she has written *Manitoba roundabout* (a travel book); *Stormy summer* (a teen-age novel in a Georgian Bay setting); *Ootook, Eskimo girl* (juvenile fiction written around her husband's photographs); *The Real book about Canada* (for young readers); *How we live in Canada;* the text for *British Columbia in pictures* (to accompany her husband's photographs); and she has contributed to the Canadian section of the *Encyclopedia of world travel.* Her book *The Luck of the La Verendryes* was prepared with the help of a Centennial Commission grant.

The products of her foreign travels are *Greece and the Greeks, China and the Chinese, The Grand Canal of China,* and *How people live in China.* A review of *China and the Chinese* says "she has a well-organized, sensible approach, and she packs every page, every sentence with facts that document the changes since the 1949 Revolution."

In addition, Mrs Harrington has written over twenty-three hundred articles, children's stories, radio dramas and talks. Lyn represented the Canadian Authors Association at the Adelaide (Australia) Festival of the Arts in 1968; one result of this excursion was her most recent book, *Australia and New Zealand.* She is currently working on a book about the polar regions.

Lyn Harrington is a small, lively and outgoing person with lots of verve. She enjoys talking about her interests and travels both informally and to groups. She intends to continue writing, at the same time trying to improve her own work and the lot of her colleagues.

June Munro
Colleges Bibliocentre, Toronto

Christie Harris

Christie Harris is an attractive vivacious woman whose grand-children are now enjoying reading her books. Born Christie Irwin in Newark, New Jersey on 2 November 1907, she moved to British Columbia with her Irish immigrant family in 1908. British Columbia is still her home province and has provided the chief source material for her writings. Her husband, Thomas Harris, is a retired immigration officer, and as her readers well know, the Harrises have five children. For the past several years they have lived in Surrey, a few miles from Vancouver.

From the beginning, Mrs Harris's writing closely paralleled her personal life. The first stories she sold, to a Vancouver newspaper, were written originally for the children she taught as an elementary school teacher before her marriage. Marriage and a family did not curtail her writing, but had rather the opposite effect. Mrs Harris continued to contribute both children's stories and humorous sketches for the women's pages of the newspaper. Later she wrote scripts and did talks in the same vein for CBC radio. When she accepted a CBC request to try some scripts for its school broadcast series, she unknowingly began to lay the groundwork for her later writing. The work demanded complete accuracy and sincerity, characteristics that are clearly evident in her writing today. Moreover stories which she uncovered but was unable to follow up as fully as she might have liked then, are providing material for some of her books now. Experience in script writing did present one problem later, when she found she had a tendency to write for the ear rather than the eye. Seven years as the women's editor of the local weekly newspaper during this time taught her to be fast as well as accurate.

Mrs Harris's first book, *Cariboo Trail,* was based directly on a school broadcast series. It deals with the Overland Trek of 1863 to the Cariboo gold fields. Her Hawthorne family is accepted more or less on sufferance by a band of trekkers, and during the wearisome and often dangerous journey, twelve year old Maeve struggles to prove that the dream she shares with her adventuresome father is not impossible for the family to fulfil.

Soon after the publication of *Cariboo Trail,* the Harrises were transferred from the Lower Mainland north to Prince Rupert. The move provided a break with her previous activities, allowing Mrs Harris to give a different direction to her writing.

The locale had a distinct bearing on her next book. Her immediate fascination with the isolated and ruggedly beautiful country and with the remaining vestiges of a once great Indian culture was reinforced by the research for a final school broadcast series on the Indians of the Northwest Coast. Particularly intrigued by their legends, Mrs Harris continued her investigations in this area, using ethnological reports and the resources of some fine local private libraries as well as compiling her own observations in trips aboard the family sailboat. The result was *Once upon a totem,* a strong collection of five legends, each chosen for its story appeal and for its portrayal of an aspect of Indian culture.

Research of a different nature went into *You have to draw the line somewhere.* This book recreates the story of her older daughter, Moira, a fashion artist. It was undertaken at Moira's suggestion, and she collaborated on its preparation with a frankness that occasionally startled the mother if not the author. It was Moira who insisted that her mother must know the fashion art scene for herself, thus Mrs Harris found herself in the peculiar position of retracing her own daughter's footsteps.

In *West with the white chiefs* Mrs Harris returned to another story that had intrigued her from school broadcast days, Dr Walter Cheadle's account of his "journey for pleasure" across Canada with Viscount Milton. Here her protagonist is a shadowy but historically real figure, the young son of Cheadle's Assiniboine guide, and it is through his eyes that we see the journey from Fort Pitt west.

A Canada Council grant enabled Mrs Harris to undertake the research necessary for her next book. An earlier attempt to pursue the story of the great Haida artist, Charles Edenshaw, had been frustrated by lack of information. Her investigations soon revealed that this was more than the account of an unusual man. Thus *Raven's cry* became the account of a family of great chiefs and artists, and indeed of a whole culture. *Raven's cry* received the Canadian Association of Children's Librarians Book of the Year for Children medal in 1967.

With *Confessions of a toe hanger*, Mrs Harris ventured once more into family collaboration to tell the story of her younger daughter, Sheilagh, the "Feeney" of the earlier book. During a year spent in Prince Edward Island where Sheilagh lives, mother and daughter worked together. The humorous but poignant account of the "ordinary" middle child in a talented family is now the favourite reading of Sheilagh's own young daughters.

In the *Forbidden frontier*, Mrs Harris dealt again with the period of the Cariboo Gold Rush. Its title is derived from Camus' *The Rebel* and it concerns the conflict between two strong-minded youngsters, Alison Stewart, half Scot, half Haida, loyalties torn between her dual ancestries, but fully at home on the frontier, and Megan Scully, an Irish immigrant girl, unaccustomed to the ways of the pioneer west.

Mrs Harris's most recent book is once again "family-based." *Let X be excitement* was written in collaboration with her eldest son, Michael (Ralph to her readers) a former Olympic oarsman, RCAF test pilot and now an aeronautical research engineer. To quote his mother's words which appear in the front of the book, "Though a born inventor, he did not invent even one incident. The truth was more than sufficient. Especially for his mother."

As to the future, there are many files of notes still remaining to be dealt with. But there is one book Mrs Harris is convinced she will never write – the mathematics text predicted in her high high school annual!

Shirley Ellison
School of Library Science
University of Alberta, Edmonton

Bibliography – Christie Harris
Cariboo trail. Longmans, 1957
Confessions of a toe hanger. McClelland, 1967
Forbidden frontier. McClelland, 1968
Once upon a totem. McClelland, 1963
Raven's cry. McClelland, 1966
West with the White Chiefs. McClelland, 1965
You have to draw the line somewhere. McClelland, 1964

Kay Hill

Children's librarians will tell you Kay Hill's prize-winning book *And tomorrow the stars* is always out! The book that won the Canadian Association of Children's Librarians medal for the Book of the Year for Children in 1969 is a fictionalized biography of John Cabot. Miss Hill traces Cabot's life from his boyhood in Genoa, to his history-making trip from Bristol, England, in quest of a new route to Asia. To obtain authentic background material she travelled extensively in Europe visiting the scenes of Cabot's early and later life: Genoa, Venice, Lisbon and Bristol, with frequent visits to archives and libraries, particularly the British Museum. A grant from the Canada Council assisted Miss Hill in her research.

Despite these travels abroad, Kay Hill is essentially a Nova Scotian, and has spent the greater part of her life in the province for which she has a great fondness. She has described it as the loveliest and most interesting spot on earth. After high school, 37 she took a business course, which eventually led her to Montreal where she worked for a time with an advertising firm. She spent several years as secretary to the Superintendent of Citadel Hill in Halifax (now a National Historic Park) – a congenial atmosphere for someone with her sense of history. She also worked at the Halifax Memorial Library, of which she has always been an enthusiastic patron. However, the urge to write was very strong and as soon as it was possible to devote full time to her craft, Miss Hill did so. She has worked as a writer for some years now with much of her material being written for radio and television.

Her writing career really began at the age of 12 when her stories appeared first in Sunday school papers. She wrote her first CBC script in 1946 – a series of radio documentaries. Her first radio play was called *Fighting Man,* with the setting a printing business. (A printing press in the firm run by Miss Hill's two brothers supplied the sound effects.) The story dealt with an ex-service man and his efforts to re-adapt to civilian life after World War II. *The Gillans,* a serial for the local CBC Farm Broadcast, was written by Miss Hill from 1948 to 1951.

The story of the vicar who schemed to get his three daughters married, with its historically accurate setting in Nova Scotia, was sold to the CBC in Halifax under the title *The Aylesford Maidens.* An expanded version was later broadcast on three different occasions, rewritten for the stage, and converted into a musical with the title *Three to Get Married.* Her radio plays were frequently heard on CBC programs *Summer Fallow, Saturday Night Theatre* and *Halifax Theatre.* Miss Hill's first television experience was in writing the serial *Mrs Byng's Boarders;* some years later she wrote another television serial *A Train of Murder* which she describes as a "real cliff-hanger."

A memorable television play was *Adele,* the story of Victor Hugo's daughter. Her tragic search for the man she loved led her to Halifax in the 1800s. Miss Hill's feeling for history was very evident in this play as she depicted the social scene in the port city of that time. Tragedy is not what she enjoys writing most, however, and her characters are usually warm and pleasant personalities, and her plots most frequently humorous. She has been described by a CBC script editor as "an editor's dream" – willing to follow suggestions and able to look objectively at her own work.

Apart from *And tomorrow the stars,* her books include a group of Indian legends written primarily for the young: *Glooscap and his magic* (published by McClelland and Stewart and also published in the United States and England); *Badger, the mischief maker;* and *More Glooscap stories.* Six of the Glooscap stories have been published in Japanese. She feels that her nieces and nephews have helped her acquire an insight into the kind of story that appeals to children and young people, and many of her earlier stories for children were "tried out" on them. In fact her family has always been a source of encouragement in her writing.

When not writing, Kay Hill is a keen amateur painter and is always anxious to capture her surroundings on canvas. She is also very interested in Scottish country dancing.

After returning from her second trip overseas to complete the Cabot research Miss Hill moved to the old town of Annapolis Royal where she occupied an apartment in the midst of what turned out to be an historic resoration project. She became involved in all the restoration activities which helped stimulate her interest in old houses.

Perhaps as a result, she has recently purchased an old house in the small fishing village of Ketch Harbour where she means to enjoy to the full her natural surroundings and the people she meets. Here, by diligent beach-combing, she has complemented her furniture with such appropriate items as a large bait-tub, in which she keeps firewood, a bo'-sun's chair used as a book rack, and fish boxes and lobster traps converted into useful furnishings. She shares the house with her cat Tinker who is a good companion and a continuous source of amusement. Being a very sociable person Miss Hill can now extend her warm hospitality to a large circle of friends. The house also gives her the opportunity to pause from the rush and bustle of life when she wishes to think through possible plots and sort out characters for her novels and plays. After a few months of country living she begrudges even a few hours spent in the city. Such surroundings should be conducive to the writing of many more articles, plays and stories to follow *And tomorrow the stars*.

Barbara B. Smith
Nova Scotia Museum Library, Halifax

R.D. Lawrence

When I first read *The Place in the forest* I felt I was visiting a never-never land, strange and lovely, and brimming with sounds and sights that most of us never hear nor see. The secret of R. D. Lawrence's genius is precisely that he does hear and see, and he is able to expose for his readers so many of nature's fascinating facets.

Actually it lies no more than one hundred miles from Toronto, this beloved Place of his – four hundred and twenty-five acres of virgin forest somewhere east of Orillia. Heré Ron Lawrence does most of his writing, but anyone arriving un-expectedly is apt to find him up a tree. Not that this cultivated man runs to arboreal gymnastics, but he might well be climbing to the aid of a sick raccoon; or, scantily attired, down on hands and knees, grubbing worms for an abandoned baby bird.

But this intensely sincere author, with dreams in his dark eyes, is much more than a nature buff. "Yes, I have written mostly of nature, but I am concerned with all things that have life – animals, birds, man, and how they are all evolving in this vast, lovely land of Canada."

His own life has been spent in many parts of the world, the seamy sides of which are well known to him. He was born in Vigo, Spain, of British parents, and he received his early education in that country. At 14 he had espoused the republican cause and was fighting in the Spanish Civil War. Later he went to England to finish his education, which was again interrupted by war, with the result that he spent the years from 1939-1945 in the British Army. For the next decade he travelled widely in Europe, Africa and the United States. In 1954 he came to Canada, and he makes it very clear that he is permanently here to stay.

Why Canada? "Because," he replied, "Europe was too confining, too crowded, and contained too many unhappy memories." In Canada he found the *lebensraum* so vital to his temperament. He spent his early days here in exploring the country from coast to coast and tried his hand at everything from cutting pulpwood in British Columbia, to highway construction jobs at 92 cents an hour, to farming in the Lake of the Woods district. By then he had developed the passionate love for, and belief in Canada that is so characteristic of this keenly observant and sensitive man.

Because he must write – "always have since I was a child" – he joined the staff of the *Toronto Star,* and subsequently the *Toronto Telegram.* Currently he publishes a weekly subsidiary of the *Telegram* in Ajax.

Although Ron Lawrence has been writing since he was a young boy in Spain, the books for which he is known throughout the world all deal with the Canadian scene. The first of these, and the one of greatest appeal to children, is *Wildlife in Canada,* published in 1966. It has received excellent reviews at home and abroad, and has been accepted as a reliable guide to the main species of wild animals that abound in Canada. The many splendid photographs in this book, and indeed in all his books, prove that Mr Lawrence is as perceptive with the camera as he is with the pen.

The Place in the forest appeared in 1967. Here Ron reveals himself not as the coldly scientific scientist, but rather as the enquiring, warmly human naturalist, deeply concerned with all of life and its evolution. Reading this book, and its sequel, *Where the water lilies grow,* we are aware of a man and his wife seeking peace and contentment, happiness, salvation, if you like, through an understanding of nature. "I learned the necessity of toleration among people by studying the habits of animals and birds. They never kill without need. Only man kills wantonly."

It is not surprising that R. D. Lawrence, with his concern for the land and all that dwells therein, should feel compelled to express himself on the subject of pollution. This he did in 1969 in his book, *The Poison makers.* It is a hard-hitting attack aimed at all of us who, in so many insidious ways, are allowing our environment to become contaminated. It is interesting to note that even before this, in 1967 and 1968, Mr Lawrence had already received the Frank H. Kortright Award for excellence in writing in the field of conservation.

Books to come? Many more, we hope, but definitely two are in progress at present. From Ron's description of these one feels he is moving in the direction of fiction – although if he does adopt this *genre* the result will be firmly based on fact. *Cry wild* is the title he has chosen for a book on wolves. Here he will be exploring the life cycle of the species as seen through the eyes of one wolf, the hero, with man the villain. To my suggestion that this seemed reminiscent of Farley Mowat, the author replied with an unequivocal "no resemblance."

As we talked together I questioned him as to why he had never written about his exciting and danger-fraught youth in Spain. "But that is just what I am doing now – that is the other book I am working on, and it will be about the days when I had to wave a white hankie to ensure a safe passage to and from school." The proposed title is *Children of blood,* but I very much doubt that it will be a sensational thriller about children too early exposed to civil strife and bloodshed because Ron Lawrence had a far-off, brooding look in his eyes as he mused, "I am tackling the problem of youth by contrasting the way life was then for young people in Spain, and how it is for young people here and now."

Beatrice Evans
Provincial Library Service, Toronto

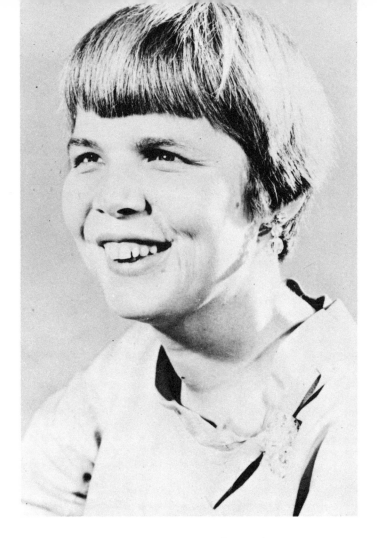

Jean Little

That anyone would consider her a very courageous person is an appalling thought to Jean Little, prize-winning author from Guelph. Throughout her life, Jean has taken the "so what!" attitude concerning her handicap, indeed she has turned it into an asset in both her work and her writing. She feels that her limited sight has merely given her greater empathy and deeper understanding of the tremendous problems that the handicapped, especially children, must face.

From her early childhood, Jean was allowed and encouraged by parents with a wisdom that won out over protectiveness to do the things that normal children delight in, even climbing trees. Born with scars on her eyes, Jean was blind until two years of age, and has since gained very limited vision in one eye.

Both her parents were physicians and medical missionaries in Taiwan, where Jean was born 2 January 1932. The Littles returned to Canada in 1939. Her father died in 1953, but her mother still maintains a strenuous practice in Guelph. Jean began her formal education there, attending public and high schools; then at the University of Toronto she received her BA in English Language and Literature, excelling not only in her class but the whole of Victoria College in 1955.

After graduation Jean's interest in the handicapped developed into a vocation through training as a teacher for children with motor handicaps at the Institute for Special Education in Salt Lake City, Utah. There, at special request, she taught a demonstration class for children with intellectual handicaps, and did some private tutoring as well.

Returning to Guelph Jean taught at the Crippled Children's Centre sponsored by the Rotary Club, has been a counsellor at Woodeden Crippled Children's Camp in Muskoka, and in 1960 was a visiting instructor in exceptional children's education at Florida State University. It was here that she completed *Mine for keeps* which won the Little, Brown Canadian Children's Book Award for 1961.

Mine for keeps is the story of a little girl's problems in adjusting to family life after spending several years in a special institution devoted to training handicapped children. Jean had searched long and hard for a book woven around the problems of cerebral palsy, or even one that dealt realistically with any crippled child, and felt there was a great need for one that was not tied up neatly at the end with a convenient miracle. Jean's young heroine Sally has the same physical handicap at the end of the book as at the beginning, but has conquered an even bigger one – fear.

Her third book *Spring begins in March,* published in 1966, is a sequel in that it deals with the same Copeland family of *Mine for keeps,* and revolves around the younger sister. Here the "problem" is Meg and her predilection for trouble. Faltering school work, relations with a crippled sister, grandmother moving in with the resultant cramped quarters and flaring arguments, even a birthday puppy that's as big a discipline problem as Meg is herself – all are interwoven in a realistic way.

Both *Spring begins in March* and *Home from far* were chosen as Junior Literary Guild selections.

Home from far, Jean's second story, deals with a completely different situation. A sister's grief over a lost twin brother killed in a traffic accident is balanced against having to accept into the family not only a foster sister but a brother as well, and one who turns out to have the same name. The parents' decision to take a positive step to adjustment is a story of family courage.

Jean feels that it is the direct result of her father's sometimes subtle, sometimes bullying encouragement, and almost psychic instinct, that she has evolved into the writer she is today. By the time she was 12, when she received her first cheque for a poem, she was incurably addicted to the thrill of seeing her words in print. She has in fact maintained her interest in poetry with the publication of *When the pie was opened,* a varied collection of poems of nature, dogs, love and imagery.

While it might appear that writing is her whole life, Jean also sketches, is an avid traveller, and an active CGIT leader. An early discovery and appreciation of the novels of Rosemary Sutcliff prompted her to write a fan letter, and from this developed a warm friendship through correspondence. In 1965, the highlight of a round-the-world trip with her mother was meeting Miss Sutcliff and visiting the home of the renowned author. Jean also has delighted in an extensive tour of Europe and Russia.

As her poetry would indicate, Jean's dogs are very important to her. The impeccable manners of the West Highland Terriers, Susie, immortalized in *Mine for keeps,* and later Robbie, acquired after the success of that novel, have made them welcome library visitors, and a delight to the children.

Another acquisition from the fruits of her writing is the cottage on Three Mile Lake near Bracebridge named "Gilead" after a favourite hymn. This is the setting of *One to grow on,* the most autobiographical of Jean's novels. In this one, her most normal heroine conquers the insidious habit of lying.

Take wing, released in 1968, deals with mental retardation. An older sister has the responsibility and care of her seven-year-old retarded brother, and Jean has handled this situation with great compassion and understanding. *Look through my window,* the story of a withdrawn only child who is used to confined apartment living, came out in 1970. The family moves to a huge abandoned mansion in a small town, hard on the heels of the temporary adoption of four exuberant cousins. Emily not only learns the rewards that come from sharing in a large family but finds Kate who becomes her first real friend.

Never one to coast on her past successes, or let her hungry young audience down, Jean Little is hard at work on future books – at least two new stories are well on their way into eager young hands and hearts!

Isobel Boggs
Guelph Public Library

James McNeill

They hear, "Once there was . . ." or "Long ago there lived . . ." and ten children know that their talented father is about to tell them another enthralling story.

James McNeill, an award-winning author of two books of folk tales from around the world, was born in Edmonton, 9 February 1925, and grew up in the Peace River area of Northern Alberta. In the 1930s books were extremely scarce, and one of the few books he remembers owning was Lamb's *Tales from Shakespeare*. This gave him a healthy respect for stories, and he says, "Up there when there was no radio and the newspaper came once a week, story telling was a real art."

During World War II, James McNeill served in the Canadian Navy as a Commando. After the war he attended business college, studied Russian, and in 1948 joined the Intelligence Corps of the Canadian Army. His exciting and varied career includes a short period as a waiter in a Chinese restaurant and a stint as a taxi dispatcher.

Retiring in 1960 to devote more time to writing, McNeill later returned to work with the Dominion Bureau of Statistics. In mid-1967 he became a Literature Development Specialist with the Department of Indian Affairs and Northern Development, specializing in the area of Eskimo studies. In his spare time he is studying Celtic and Slavic folklore.

Why did he decide to write books for children? As Hugh Lofting, another soldier-author, did before him, James McNeill began by telling stories to a delighted but critical audience, his own family. He says that his children are his best critics and if the story is dull they will show their distaste by going to sleep!

While doing research at the Library of Congress in Washington for the Canadian Army, Staff Sgt McNeill decided to find a story he had heard as a child. From this research came, not the story he sought, but a wealth of material which resulted in a book of folk tales from around the world, *The sunken city*. McNeill tested all his stories on his children. His wife wrote them as he told them.

"In Holland, beneath the waves of the Zuider Zee, lie the ruins of a once prosperous city called Stavoren." Thus begins the title story of his first book. Few of the tales are familiar, perhaps only "The Three wishes," a story from Hungary of a wife who wishes that a sausage were attached to her husband's nose. The most unusual story is the beautiful "Haunted forest from Lithuania." It is the tale of Elspeth who flees from the cruel treatment of an evil stepmother to find happiness in a haunted forest with a group of immortal beings.

He recreates for Canadian children, in a simple but evocative and witty style, stories from lands whose people have added so richly to our culture. Therein one finds stories of knights, dragons, princesses, all the magic of Europe and Asia. The book is delightfully illustrated by Theo Dimson and won an honour award in the Hans Christian Andersen International Competition in Europe in 1962.

His second book, *The Double knights,* won the Canadian Association of Children's Librarians medal in 1966. This is a book with an international flavour, containing 17 stories from Europe, Mexico, Trinidad, Japan, Russia, India and Africa. Unlike the first collection which concentrates on princesses, mermaids and dragons, *The Double knights* centres around tricksters, clever men, giant killers and trolls. The illustrations, also by Theo Dimson, fit the stronger, more realistic idiom of these stories.

His work for the Department of Indian Affairs and Northern Development consists of teaching individual Eskimo people the art of creative writing both in their own language and in English. He has collected folktales from the native people of the Mackenzie River and has published the first book in the Eskimo language for recreational reading. A highlight of his work is the publication of the first genuine Eskimo novel in the world written by Markoosie. An English version of this, translated by the author, *Harpoon of the Hunter,* was published in the autumn of 1970. He has edited several life stories of Canadian Indians, and has inaugurated a new magazine, *Tawow.* During the winter of 1969-70 Mr McNeill wrote 80 scripts of stories of the Indian and Eskimo peoples for the CBC.

He hopes in the near future to publish at least two more books of folk tales, one devoted to Siberian Eskimo folklore, and one centred around legends of the Indian cultural heroes.

Mr McNeill's books are a welcome addition to our collections of folk tales. He is truly a twentieth-century minstrel.

Marilyn McCulloch
Ottawa Public Library

Josephine Phelan

Josephine Phelan has an absorbing interest in history, a capacity for study and research, the ability to see people and situations as they are, a creative, inquiring mind untrammelled by routine approaches and attitudes, and the urge and ability to write.

Her first book, *The Ardent exile,* published in 1951, is a biography of D'Arcy McGee whose major role in bringing about confederation in Canada was cut short by his assassination. D'Arcy McGee emerges as a vital person, and the events of his time are related with a freshness and immediacy that make these times a part of the reader's own experience. For this work Miss Phelan received the 1952 Governor-General's literary award for creative non-fiction as well as the 1952 University of British Columbia award for popular biography.

Miss Phelan was born in Hamilton, Ontario in 1905 and grew up in Guelph. Matriculation at the Loretto Convent there led to a Knights of Columbus Fellowship which she held while attending St Michael's College, University of Toronto. She graduated with an honours degree in modern history and won the Alexander MacKenzie Fellowship. With this she took her M.A. in history at the same university. She attended the Ontario College of Education and taught in a high school for a short time. After post graduate work in history at the University of Wisconsin she worked for two years with the Renouf Publishing Company in Montreal. In 1943 Miss Phelan received her Bachelor of Library Science degree from the Library School, University of Toronto, and joined the staff of the Toronto Public Library.

Her urge to write is powerful and her second book, published in 1954, is a novel for young people, *The Boy who ran away* – to the Hudson's Bay Company territory. In 1956 she published *The Bold heart*, the story of Father Lacombe. Her latest book, *The Ballad of D'Arcy McGee*, was published in the fall of 1967 in the Great Stories of Canada series. About the same person as *The Ardent exile* it is written with fresh interest and appeal. A review appeared in the Winter 1968 issue of *In Review*.

While working as a librarian Miss Phelan belonged to the Canadian Library Association and the Ontario Library Association. When the Young People's Section of the Canadian Library Association was preparing *Standards of work with young people in Canadian public libraries,* later published as an occasional paper by the Association, Miss Phelan wrote the chapter, "Young people and public libraries." In this chapter she expressed clearly and succinctly the relation of young people to the public library. She said librarians need to realize that while young people are part of the public using the library they come to the library as individuals with individual needs.

In 1965 Josephine Phelan retired from the Toronto Public Library, but she is far from "retired." A four-month trip to Europe during which she lived in Paris for six weeks was just the beginning of an active career. She remarks that she used to work five days a week (in the library) but now she works seven! She is a member of the Canadian Authors Association and is often asked to speak; this she does with wit and enjoyment. Her membership in the United Empire Loyalist Association brings her in close touch with an interesting period of Canadian history. A feature article on D'Arcy McGee set on the centre spread of the 6 April 1968 *Globe Magazine* appeared the day before its subject had been killed one hundred years before. Her current work in progress is an historical biography of William Warren Baldwin, father of Robert Baldwin. This work was interrupted by a research job which will probably be finished in 1971, and then Miss Phelan expects to concentrate on her book. We hope that she has no more interruptions for we look forward to it with interest and anticipation.

Isabel Bevis

Dorothy
M. Reid

On 31 December 1967 an active love affair of 21 years was seemingly ending. That was when Dorothy M. Reid retired as head of the children's department of the then Fort William Public Library (which has since become the Brodie Street Branch of the Thunder Bay Public Library). Her active involvement in a three-cornered romance with books, people and libraries was supposedly over. For it was in 1946, in the Northern Ontario mining town of Geraldton, that a life-long love of books and people bore fruit. The town council, having seen some of her poetry in print, appointed her to the first Geraldton Public Library Board.

Staff was scarce up there. Few people knew much about books or reading. So Mrs Reid agreed to work temporarily as the librarian until the Board could hire someone else. That temporary job became as temporary as the famous temporary buildings in Ottawa. Both Geraldton and Fort William were fortunate when she agreed to work until the Board could find someone else. Because they were never able to.

In September 1956 the Reids moved to Fort William where she soon became the children's librarian. This move was the result, in part, of the Irish blandishments of Mike Donovan. And so you had Irish and Scot showing the rest of the world how to run an excellent library.

For Dorothy was born in Edinburgh many years ago. An only child, orphaned at four, she went to live with one aunt and five bachelor uncles, who roamed the various parts of the world, passing the child and aunt among themselves – a nomadic existence by today's standards, perhaps a lonely one in some respects. Yet it was here that Dorothy learned about the meaning of books by watching her aunt and uncles read. She became accustomed to finding solace and laughter and companionship in books. World War I took the lives of her five uncles, and Dorothy came to Canada with her aunt and her aunt's husband.

For a while they lived in Weyburn, Saskatchewan, where she attended school. Later, Dorothy attended Normal School and became a teacher in one of the many one-room schools that have dotted the prairies for so many decades. It was here that she married Jack Reid and went to live on a half section on the prairie.

No appreciation of Dorothy Reid would be worth a pinch of salt if it failed to mention Jack Reid. Tall in stature, he was a giant in the multitude of small ways it takes to be a human being. He shared her love of nature, her love of birds and animals. Meeting them together, one could see the truth of the cliché "her tower of strength." His tragic death in 1965 took the excitement from the award that that year brought, when Dorothy was presented the medal of the Canadian Association of Children's Librarians for *The Tales of Nanabozho.*

This book dates back to 1940, when Jack decided that eight years of drought, stem rust, and grasshoppers was enough. So he moved his family of four to the gold town of Geraldton. It was here that, between the births of two more children, Dorothy first heard about Nanabozho from Indian story tellers. These stories, with their understanding of nature, respect for animals, and the cussed humanity of their hero, struck a chord that eventually resulted in her book.

The Geraldton years came and went, and at the end of that period the family moved again. This time to Fort William, where Dorothy was going to be the young people's librarian. A sudden resignation, and she was head of the children's department from 1957 to 1967 when the department increased its circulation by over ninety-nine thousand volumes. For over ten years, Mrs Reid flew *The Magic Carpet* from one of the local radio stations every Sunday morning, telling stories on the air to children – and their parents.

The last few years have seen the rest of Canada recognize her unique talents. Besides giving her awards for her writing, she was judge on the Centennial Commission's competition for children's books. In 1967, she was the patron of Young Canada's Book Week. Her knowledge of books was put to work in 1966 when she was asked to act on *In Review*'s first advisory committee.

At the time of her retirement, some nostalgic words were written about the love affair ending, as life was taking another of its twists and turns. The idea that she would find a quiet retreat on the banks of the Kaministiquia, visited by birds, flying squirrels, deer and a friendly family of skunks was felt to be chimerical. Less than six months after her retirement she was being importuned to return to work, this time in the adult department, on a part-time basis and only for a little while.

Her new duties consist of being in charge of acquisitions of the library as well as rigorously weeding the adult circulating collection. Dorothy also provides the supervision needed for Sunday opening. Part-time work?

If working in the library again is not enough, she has made several forays into the United States, addressing librarians, library school students, education students and children at Duluth, Minneapolis and the University of Minneapolis. Each sortie is prefaced with comments like "Why did I ever agree" and are concluded with "It was so much fun."

Working part-time and lecturing part-time didn't prove to be enough so over the winter she has worked on two more books. One is tentatively being called *Adventures of Wisakedjak,* about the hero-spirit of the Cree Indians, like Glooscap of the Abnaki and Nanabozho of the Ojibways. The other book is a more personal story being called *Garlanded with disasters*.

But do words adequately capture the spirit of a warm personality? How do you emphasize the natural warmth, the bubbling enthusiasm, the gay lilt which help to carry everyone along with her? Do words bring out the feeling of youthfulness? A librarian has said that the Brodie Street Library is fortunate in having so many young people like Dorothy Reid on staff. These words try to sum up the magic of Dorothy; a person whom it is easy to admire, who is shy but bold for what she thinks right, wonderful to know and work with.

Peter Mutchler
Thunder Bay Public Library

Kerry Wood

The Red Deer River rises near Lake Louise in Banff National Park and flows eastward through the foothills and out across beautiful parkland before cutting through the strange, fascinating Bad Lands on its way to join the South Saskatchewan River. In the parkland just half way between Calgary and Edmonton at a ford in the river the first settlement of the present city of Red Deer began. This is Kerry Wood's home, and he and the river cannot be separated. He has lived near it most of his life, explored it, fished it, and been dumped into it from a tippy canoe.

Kerry Wood was born in New York City on 2 June 1907 of Scottish parents. When he was a year old the family moved to Canada and came west in 1910 to Manitoba, then to Saskatchewan for a year, and finally to Alberta where they settled in Red Deer in 1918. This has been his home ever since. His interest in nature and his constant questions about birds and animals led to his membership in the Alberta Natural History Society as one of its youngest members when he was 12 years old.

From natural history it was a short step to the early history of the area. Many of the old timers were still alive and they had many a story to tell of the early days. He was particularly interested in David Thompson, and he has told about him in *The Map-maker*. The people of Rocky Mountain House invited Kerry to their celebration of the opening of the David Thompson Highway to do a broadcast. The first 20 minutes was on the history of Rocky Mountain House and another 20 minutes was to be broadcast from an aeroplane flying over the David Thompson Route. Later he sent this tape, with an account of the event, to David Thompson's great-grandson in Toronto who told him he couldn't tell that the last 12 minutes were done in Kerry's basement with the vacuum cleaner simulating the noise of the aeroplane – bad weather had forced the plane to land before they could finish.

At a very early age, Kerry decided that he was going to be a writer. When he was 16 his parents moved to Vancouver, and he was left behind to finish his high school year. Instead of following them at all, he decided to stay and begin his writing career. He had little money and for the next two years he lived off the land. His book, *Wild winter,* describes part of that ordeal. He haunted the public library and the librarian helped him find out what native plants the Indians used for food and their trapping methods; three times he nearly starved to death. At last a story was accepted and appeared in *Western Home Monthly*.

As assistant Scout Master at 18, he began telling stories around camp fires and the boys clamoured for more. This response gave him the idea of publishing them, and for five years *Boys Life Magazine* published his *Wild Bill Bumps* stories. About this time he was also local reporter for the *Edmonton Bulletin* and later wrote for the *Calgary Albertan* and the *Edmonton Journal*. Mr Wood says he has been writing for 47 years and publishing for 45 years. He has written 18 books, one of which, *Cowboy yarns* was runner-up for the Canadian Book of the Year for Children medal. Another interesting book is *A Time for fun; a guide to hobbies and handicrafts,* published in 1967. In this book he deals with the great variety of artistic shapes to be found in driftwood and mountain juniper and how to finish them; also how to make Indian bows and arrows, humming bird feeders, bird houses; tips on outdoor cookery and camping, to name but a few. He writes from his own experience and has many fine examples of his handiwork in his home. He is still writing books and a new one is due shortly. All together, aside from books, Kerry Wood has published over six thousand short stories and over seven thousand articles other than the weekly newspaper articles since 1930. He had a program on CBC from 1939 to 1966 and he still broadcasts nature talks over CKUA Edmonton on Sunday mornings. He has also to his credit 137 TV scripts for the CBC

National network and 174 TV personal appearances for the Western Network of the CBC.

Kerry and his wife, Marjory, have been married for 35 years. Though the first five years were in the "Dirty Thirties" and they had a very rough time, Kerry is proud of the fact that they were never on relief; he says his Scottish stubbornness wouldn't let him. Once, when they were down to 15 cents, his wife said, "Don't worry, there is a star over you." Her faith was justified for the next day a cheque arrived from the *Reader's Digest*. Now they have a comfortable home about eight miles east of Red Deer on 40 acres of parkland bordering, of course, on the Red Deer River and surrounded by all the things close to a nature lover's heart. They have three children – two daughters and a son. The elder daughter, Rondo, works with the Ontario Institute for Studies in Education in Toronto; Heather went to Oxford on a scholarship studying for her PhD in Comparative Religions and Intellectual History. She married in Oxford in July 1969 and is now living in London, England. Their son Gregory is now 22 and works in Edmonton.

Though the people of Red Deer were hostile at first to the young man who dared to be "different," they now have honoured him by naming a street in the city after him, and they held a Kerry Wood Day and presented him with a city-crest ring. As a result of his book, *The Great chief,* a large area of Central Alberta has been designated as "Maskepetoon Boy Scout Area" with part of it the "Kerry Wood District." The County of Red Deer also created a nature park called Maskepetoon Park, and the city calls its large recreational area "Great Chief Park." In 1965 Kerry Wood was given the Alberta Historical Award.

Kerry Wood's Centennial project is a personalized history of the Red Deer River Country called *A Corner of Canada* which is illustrated with his own sketches. Again, he and the river cannot be separated because this very interesting book is also a reflection of Kerry Wood.

Dorothy Morgan
Calgary Public Library